To the reader:

Welcome to the DK ELT Graded Readers! These readers are different. They explore aspects of the world around us: its history, geography, science … and a lot of other things. And they show the different ways in which people live now, and lived in the past.

These DK ELT Graded Readers give you material for reading for information, and reading for pleasure. You are using your English to do something real. The illustrations will help you understand the text, and also help bring the Reader to life. There is a glossary to help you understand the special words for this topic. Listen to the cassette or CD as well, and you can really enter the world of the Olympic Games, the *Titanic*, or the Trojan War … and a lot more. Choose the topics that interest you, improve your English, and learn something … all at the same time.
Enjoy the series!

To the teacher:

This series provides varied reading practice at five levels of language difficulty, from elementary to FCE level:
BEGINNER
ELEMENTARY A
ELEMENTARY B
INTERMEDIATE
UPPER INTERMEDIATE
The language syllabus has been designed to suit the factual nature of the series, and includes a wider vocabulary range than is usual with ELT readers: language linked with the specific theme of each book is included and glossed.
The language scheme, and ideas for exploiting the material (including the recorded material) both in and out of class are contained in the Teacher's Resource Book.
We hope you and your students enjoy using this series.

Dorling  Kindersley

LONDON, NEW YORK, SYDNEY, DELHI,
PARIS, MUNICH & JOHANNESBURG

Originally published as Eyewitness Reader
Tiger Tales in 2000 and adapted as an
ELT Graded Reader for
Dorling Kindersley by

studio **cactus** ⓒ

13 SOUTHGATE STREET WINCHESTER HAMPSHIRE SO23 9DZ

Published in Great Britain by
Dorling Kindersley Limited
9 Henrietta Street, London WC2E 8PS

2 4 6 8 10 9 7 5 3 1

Copyright © 2000
Dorling Kindersley Limited, London

A CIP catalogue record for this book is
available from the British Library.

ISBN 0-7513-2922-3

Colour reproduction by Colourscan, Singapore
Printed and bound in China by
L. Rex Printing Co., Ltd
Text film output by Chimera TRT, UK

The publisher would like to thank the following
for their kind permission to reproduce their photographs:
c=centre; t=top; b=below; l=left; r=right

Animals Animals: Zig Leszczynski 10–11, 12–13; A & M
Shah 14–15; Anup Shah 21; **Ardea London Ltd**: Arthus
Bertrand 38-39; **BBC Natural History Unit**: John
Downer 29b; Vivek Menon 20br; Lynn Stone 47tr; **Care
for the Wild International**: 10c; **Mary Evans Picture
Library**: 7tr; **Oxford Scientific Films**: Norbert Rosing
39tr; **Planet Earth Pictures**: Tom Brakefield 13tr; Richard
Matthews 22–23; Jonathan Scott 28t.

Jacket credit: **Dave King**

See our complete catalogue at
www.dk.com

Contents

ELT Graded Readers

ELEMENTARY B

TIGERS
AND BIG CATS

Written by Susan Woolard

Series Editor Susan Holden

A Dorling Kindersley Book

Tigers in Danger

In a dark rainforest in Malaysia, a tiger was standing quietly, waiting under the tall trees. The tiger was listening carefully, and was standing very still. He could hear strange noises, but he didn't know what they were. This was something new for the jungle tiger – the noise of heavy traffic. Cars, buses, and big lorries were driving along the new road through the forest. This road went along the side of the jungle, and it was now much easier for people to travel from one side of the country to the other side. But the new road also brought people and traffic much nearer to the wild animals in the rainforest.

The tiger was far away from his usual places, and he was trying to get back to his own hunting ground. He walked forwards, slowly and carefully through the trees and, as he walked, the strange noises got louder and louder.

Suddenly, the tiger stopped. Now he was in the open and there were no trees or long grass to stand in – only the bright light of the sun, high up in the sky. The tiger was surprised, and closed his eyes a little. Then he moved out into the sunlight, and into danger. He wasn't in the forest now, he was on the busy road! The frightened tiger didn't understand, and could not stop. He knew what to do in the forest, that was his territory, but he didn't know what to do here. So, he made the biggest mistake of his life and walked forwards – he did not turn back into the tall trees.

The tiger could feel the danger and he was moving faster now. He ran to the middle of the road – straight into the traffic. All the cars, buses, and lorries were travelling fast, and many of the drivers did not even see the tiger. Then there was a loud crash, and the driver of a bus jumped in surprise. He put his foot quickly down on his brake, but it was too late. The bus crashed into the tiger and killed him. One more tiger was dead.

The traffic behind the bus had to slow down, and many people stopped to help the driver. The noise got louder and louder as drivers sounded their horns, and for some time there was a traffic jam. Some of the men helped the bus driver to carry the body of the tiger to the side of the road. It was too big and heavy for one man. Then the traffic started to move quickly along the road again.

But the body of the tiger did not stay by the side of the road for very long. In the next twenty-four hours, parts of the body were taken away. Of course, this usually happens in the jungle, where a dead body means food for the other animals. But this time the body was not taken by hungry animals, it was taken by people. They knew exactly what they wanted, and they took the tiger's claws, its teeth, and its whiskers.

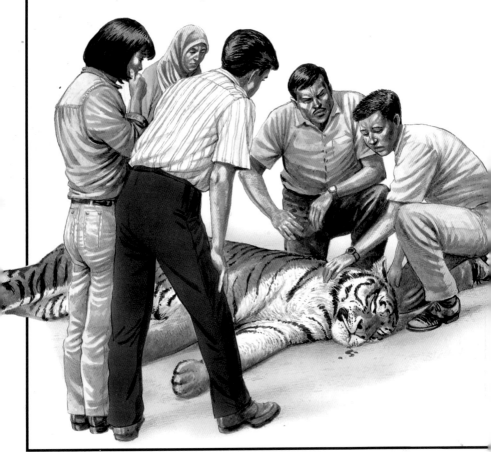

Why did the people take parts of the tiger's body? The simple answer is "money".

Some thieves steal parts of tigers to sell – and they can get a lot of money for them. But who buys tiger parts, and what do they do with them? One big market is in China, where the parts of some animals, for example the tiger, are used to make traditional medicines. People in China have used animals and plants to make medicine like this for thousands of years. In the past, it was easier to get the animals and plants, but now it is much more difficult – the number of wild animals is getting smaller, and in many countries it is illegal to kill tigers. Because it is difficult, some people today will pay a lot of money for this medicine.

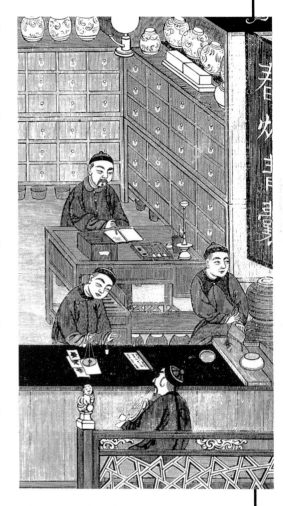

Traditional medicine
Chinese medicine uses most parts of the tiger, and different parts can help different illnesses. Many people think that the whiskers stop toothache and that the brain can stop you feeling lazy.

In most countries in the world, and this is also true in China, it is against the law to buy and sell tigers. But this does not stop the thieves, because there is a big market for traditional Chinese medicines in some other parts of the world. It can be very difficult to stop the killing – the thieves can move very quickly to kill the tiger, cut off the parts they want, and then get away before anyone sees them. Every day, at least one tiger is killed, and now the number of tigers in the world is getting smaller and smaller. Tigers are in serious danger.

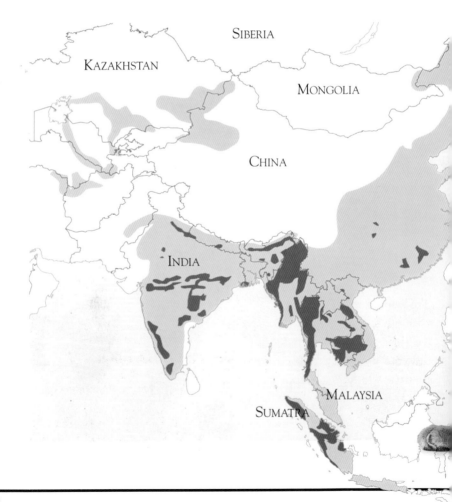

The world situation, and this danger to tigers, is clear when we look at tiger numbers. At the beginning of the twentieth century, there were about 100,000 tigers in the world. They lived in the wild in many different countries, as you can see on the map below. Today, tigers have disappeared from many of these areas. Now there are only about 6,000 living in the wild. They live in the forests and grasslands of Asia – from the far east of Russia to the west of India, and from Sumatra in the south to China in the north.

RUSSIA

Where tigers may be found today.

Where tigers lived 100 years ago.

Tigers are magnificent creatures, and it would be terrible if there were no tigers in the world in the future – in other words, if they were extinct. Luckily, many people fear this, and they are working hard to help save the tigers left in the world.

It is difficult for individual people working alone to solve all the problems, so many people join wildlife organisations. In this way, they can send money and expert help where it is needed. One organisation in Britain that tries to help the tiger is called Care for the Wild International. This organisation helps to make safe places for the tigers to live in, called reserves. These reserves are different from zoos because they are in the kinds of places where tigers live naturally – like the jungles of Malaysia and the grasslands of Africa. The animals can move about freely in the reserves, and can live in a natural way. They are not locked up in cages like animals in a zoo.

One example of the work of this organisation is a story from Cambodia, in South East Asia. Here, Care for the Wild International helped to save some tiger cubs.

One day, a mother tiger was out hunting for food for herself and her two young cubs. While she was away, some thieves came and stole her two cubs from their den (the name for a tiger's home). The thieves wanted to take the tiger cubs to the nearby country of Vietnam to sell them. The thieves had to be careful, and move quickly, because there were wildlife protection officers in the area.

A wildlife protection officer's job is to look after the wild animals in the area, and to try to stop the thieves. Luckily, this time they stopped the men, and they found the two young cubs. The police took the men away, but they were worried about the young tigers. They couldn't take the cubs back to the mother, and so they quickly took them to an animal rescue centre, where someone would look after them.

Tiger cubs

Tiger cubs drink their mother's milk when they are born. When they are about two months old, their mother starts to give them meat to eat.

When Care for the Wild International heard about the tiger cubs they sent two of their expert vets to help look after them. (Vets are animal doctors: the full name is veterinary surgeon.) At first, the cubs were very ill – they were very thin and their legs were not straight. They had a disease called rickets, which is caused by a bad diet – the tiger cubs were not getting enough good food to help them grow strong. The people in the animal rescue centre gave the cubs names. They called them Map and Tomi (many people were called these names in the local language), and the cubs became big favourites at the centre.

Very slowly, the tiger cubs grew stronger and stronger as the vets and the people in the centre looked after them. At first they fed the cubs milk, and then after a few months they started to give them meat. When they were six months old, the tiger cubs were eating more than one kilogram of meat a day.

In the wild, tiger cubs usually stay with their mother for about two years. This is a very important time for the young cubs, because it is the time when they learn how to hunt and kill other animals for food. When they are about five months old, they start to learn how to find food. At first they stay near their home, where they can "help" their mother in small ways. They run into the long grass near their den and frighten small animals. These animals run out of the grass into the open, and the mother tiger can jump on them and kill them. Then, after they are about seven months old, the tiger cubs move away from the den and start to go everywhere with their mother. They watch her very carefully, and copy what she does. In this way, they learn to hunt for themselves. When they are old enough and strong enough, they can go away from their mother and hunt alone.

Sadly, this will not happen to Map and Tomi, the two tiger cubs in the story. They can never go back into the jungle to live and hunt alone because they don't have a tiger mother to teach them how to hunt. They will grow up with humans and they will be fed by humans. A human can't show them how to hunt and survive in the wild.

But this does not mean that they will have to stay in a zoo, or that they will die. There is a future for tigers like Map and Tomi. Organisations like Care for the Wild International can take them to one of their special animal reserves. This is almost like their natural home, but there are people there to help look after them and give them food. In fact, Map and Tomi were put on a reserve with an older tigress (a female tiger) to help look after them. With this extra help, the young tigers could hunt and find food – and they have survived.

Tiger Terror

One quiet evening in January, a young man was washing his clothes in the garden behind his home. His day's work was finished, and he was alone in the garden. The man lived just outside a national park in Thailand, Southeast Asia. National parks are areas like reserves, where the animals can move freely, but there are people and organisations in the park to protect and help them.

It was very quiet in the garden, when suddenly there was a loud noise in the trees. The animals there were making the noise, and they were very frightened. Immediately, the man knew he was in danger. He dropped the clothes that he was washing, turned round, and started to run towards his house. He was frightened and moved quickly, but it was too late, and he never reached the door.

There was another noise – louder and nearer this time – and the branches of a tree broke and crashed to the ground. Suddenly, a huge tiger, nearly two metres long, jumped out of the trees and onto the man. It pushed him down to the ground and bit its teeth into his right hand. The man thought he was going to die. He was terrified!

The tiger did not kill the man immediately. The huge animal began to pull the man along the ground, towards the trees. There was a lot of blood coming from his hand and it was very painful. The man tried to pull his hand away from the tiger, and all the time he was shouting loudly for help. He was sure now that he was going to die!

Luckily, a friend was working nearby and he heard the shouts. He ran to help the man, but the tiger started to attack him too. Now the two men were terrified and in danger.

The two men shouted and screamed, but they knew the situation was bad. The tiger was big and strong enough to kill both of them. This time the park officers heard them shouting. Soon some officers arrived with guns and fired them up into the air. They wanted to help the men, but they didn't want to kill the tiger. The noise of the guns was enough to frighten the tiger away. It stopped attacking the men, and ran back into the trees. Quickly, the park officers took the men to a doctor and they survived – they lived to tell their friends their big cat story.

Eyesight
Like other big cats, tigers can see very well in the dark. They like to hunt in the early morning, late in the evening, or at night when they can surprise their prey.

Stories like this one are frightening, and many people think that the tiger is a big danger to humans. They think that tigers like to hunt and kill people all the time. But this is not really true. Tigers that are strong and healthy do not usually attack humans – they can find better, tastier meals in the wild! And humans often mean trouble – especially if they have guns. However, if a tiger is ill or injured, it may be different. It is easier for a tiger to kill a human than to kill another animal. Humans are slow and easy to catch. The tiger that attacked the two men in Thailand was probably old and weak, and very hungry. In the end, the tiger was lucky to get away from the men and get back into the jungle. The tiger seems like the dangerous and frightening one, but, in fact, people are usually much more dangerous than tigers.

When a tiger is healthy, it doesn't need to hunt humans. It is a magnificent hunter, and can kill animals that are much bigger and heavier than itself – even young rhinos and elephants can be hunted and killed by tigers. These bigger animals are important because it takes a lot of meat to feed a hungry tiger.

Tigers can eat about thirty kilograms of meat in one night – and that is a huge amount of food! But luckily, they don't need a big meal like this every day, just once or twice a week is enough. This is a good thing for the tiger, because hunting is not always easy. Although it is a good hunter, a tiger doesn't usually kill every time it hunts, in fact it only kills its prey (the animal it is hunting) about one in every fifteen hunts.

Rhinos and elephants do not come near very often. Tigers usually hunt medium-sized jungle animals like deer and wild boar (a kind of wild pig). Between hunts, and these big meals, the tigers have smaller meals, or snacks. Then they may eat fish, lizards, or turtles, and sometimes they eat insects like locusts or enjoy fruit from the trees. They also eat grass and mud, and this helps them to digest their food.

Tiger teeth
A tiger's teeth are really very good for catching, killing, and eating. Some of the teeth make holes, some hold the meat, some bite and slice, and others grind food into small pieces.

If they can, tigers like to live and hunt far away from humans. Humans are not the tiger's usual food, and they are often dangerous, especially if they are animal thieves and have guns. But the problem is that people now live too near the tiger's home in the wild, and it is very difficult (perhaps impossible) for the tiger to stay far away from people.

It seems like the tiger's world is getting smaller. In the last hundred years, people have moved into the forests and wild areas – and that means they have moved nearer and nearer to the tigers. They have destroyed large parts of the world's rainforests to make farms and to build roads, houses, and factories. So every year, the area of rainforest for the tiger to live in gets smaller and smaller. And it is not only the area to live in that is the problem. The number of wild animals living in the forest also gets smaller, so hunting is more and more difficult and there isn't enough food for the tiger to eat. Because of this, the hungry tigers have to hunt nearer and nearer to people's homes and work. The tiger has to find food to survive, and of course this can lead to a lot of serious problems.

Territory
Tigers mark out an area of the forest to live and hunt in. This is called their territory, and the tiger stops other animals hunting there. A tiger's territory can be hundreds of square kilometres.

One example of an area of rainforest that is getting smaller and smaller is the rainforest of Sumatra in Indonesia. Here, as in other parts of the world, people have cut down many of the trees. Sadly, a large part of the forest has already gone. It is possible that in the future there will be no rainforest left in Sumatra. But some people can see these dangers and they are trying to stop this before it is too late. They have started to plant new, young trees to help the forest grow again. This is called reforestation (putting the forest back again).

Unfortunately, working on the reforestation project can be a dangerous job, because the people have to work in the forests, near the tigers and other wild animals. One day, while they were busy planting young trees in Sumatra, the workers heard a noise in the trees behind them. They looked round towards the noise, and suddenly a huge tiger jumped out. It was hungry, and angry at all the strange people in its territory. The tiger attacked and it killed three men and injured three more.

After that, many of the workers were frightened and they didn't go back to work – the reforestation project was cancelled. Sadly, the tiger frightened away the people who were trying to help it. But now the work is continuing, and more people are in the forest planting young trees.

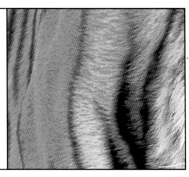

Camouflage
When an animal's coat is the colour of the area beside it, we call this camouflage. A tiger's coat is striped, and this makes it difficult to see in the forest and long grass.

Let us go Free

Big cats like lions are proud and magnificent animals, and it is often sad to see them locked up in a zoo. Although it is wonderful to see the animals, it can look like they are in a prison, walking up and down in their cage. We know that their situation in the zoo is very different from their life in the wild. These lions will probably never go back to the big, open spaces of their natural home again – the grasslands of Africa.

Many of these animals were born in the zoo, and have never seen their natural home. Perhaps, for some of the older lions, the zoo is now their only home. They don't know how to hunt, and if there were no humans to give them food they would soon die. But some people work hard to take lions out of zoos and put them back in the wild. This is difficult work, and it is only possible if the lions are very young, and they have not lived for a long time with humans. They need to be young enough to learn how to live in the wild, and how to hunt to survive.

One person who works with lions in this way is a man called Gareth Patterson. Gareth lives and works with lions in southern Africa. For many years he has worked with a small group of lions. He tries to teach them how to survive in the wild – how to stay away from danger, and how to hunt and catch other animals for food. Then, when they are ready, he helps them to go back there and live naturally in the wild. But the work is difficult, and the stories of these lions are often sad. They can teach us a lot about the dangers for lions and other animals living in the wild in Africa today.

This is the story of a lioness (a female lion) and her three young cubs. They were in danger, and Gareth Patterson helped to save them and to look after them.

In the grasslands of Africa, a lioness woke up early one morning and looked down at her three cubs. They were only five days old and they couldn't do anything for themselves. They needed their mother. They could move around a little, but their eyes were still closed. Usually, a young lion opens its eyes when it is about two weeks old.

The lioness was alone with the cubs. Before they were born, she lived with a group of other lions (this big group of lions is called a pride). Then, when it was time for the cubs to be born, she left the other lions. The lioness knew that her cubs were safer alone with her, in a place where she could stay with them and look after them. Other animals, and especially other lions, could be a danger. Sometimes, the bigger, stronger lions in the pride were very rough and careless, and it was easy for them to hurt and perhaps kill a young cub. Here, alone in their den with their mother, the cubs were safer – the other lions couldn't hurt them.

Usually, hunting was not a problem. The lioness liked to hunt animals like zebra or gazelle with the other lions. When they worked together and helped each other it was easier to catch and kill their prey. But now she was hunting alone, and it was much more difficult. The lioness was tired from looking after the cubs, so this time she didn't go after a wild animal, she killed a cow on a farm nearby – it was much easier. Later that day, the angry farmer took his gun, found the lioness and killed her. The cubs were now alone and in a lot of danger.

Luckily, the lion cubs were not alone for a long time. Some people who lived in the area found them and took them home. They gave them names, and called the male cub Batian (the same name as a local mountain). The two female cubs were called Rafiki and Furaha. These names mean "friend" and "joy" in Swahili, the language of the local people.

The people knew they couldn't keep the cubs at home, and so they took them to a man called George Adamson. Many people in the area knew about Adamson, because he liked to look after lions in danger and take them back to the wild. But this time the cubs did not stay with Adamson very long, because not long after the cubs arrived, he was killed. Living and working with the lions can be a dangerous job – not because of the lions, but because of the people who try to kill them. Adamson was killed by animal thieves – men who got money for killing lions and selling the bodies. This is illegal, but like killing and selling tigers, it is possible to make a lot of money.

After Adamson was killed, the three young cubs were in danger again. This time, Gareth Patterson took the three young lion cubs to look after them.

George Adamson

In the 1960s, someone made a film about George and his wife Joy, and their work with lions in Africa. The name of the film was *Born Free*.

Gareth Patterson took the three cubs, Batian, Rafiki, and Furaha, to a place in southern Africa called the Tuli bushlands. (Bushlands are areas of long grass and small bushes or trees.) He looked after the lions there, and watched them growing bigger and stronger. One day, Batian was tired of the usual games and the daily life with Patterson. He was growing up and he wanted to find a mate (a female lion), so he went away from his sisters. Batian travelled with a group of lionesses, and soon he was far away from home. Now he was alone, with no-one to help him.

Batian was hungry, but he didn't know anything about this strange area around him. Gareth Patterson was teaching the cubs how to survive, but after living with humans, Batian wasn't a very good hunter. The sun went down, and it started to get dark. Where was the food? Then Batian heard a noise. It was the sound of animals far away – the sound of hyenas and jackals. They were excited, and they were eating. Perhaps there was a lot of meat – enough for Batian. He listened very carefully, and his ears moved towards the sound. He was hungry, and maybe this was an easy meal. Batian started moving quickly towards his dinner.

Like all lions, Batian had a very good sense of smell – much better than a human. Soon he could smell the body of a dead animal – and it was delicious! He was feeling hungrier and hungrier. He followed his nose and moved faster and faster. It wasn't difficult to follow the smell through the long grass. Finally, Batian found what he wanted. He was right, it was the body of a dead animal – a dead donkey. But it was all very strange. The donkey was tied to a tree. He could hear the noise of the jackals and hyenas. But where were they? He couldn't see them.

Batian couldn't see them because they weren't there! The sound was coming from a loudspeaker. It was a trap, and Batian walked straight into it, because he hadn't got enough experience of life in the wild. Now there was no way out.

Suddenly, there was the sound of a gun and Batian fell to the ground. There was no time to move. Batian was killed by a bullet in the head, and he was only three years old.

Who put the body of the donkey under the tree, and why? A professional hunter and a tourist were standing near the loudspeaker, watching Batian. Their trap was very simple, but it worked.

They used the smell of a dead animal, and the sound of hungry wild dogs, to bring the big hunters (like the lions) to them. And a lion was a good catch for their day's work. The men were very happy.

Probably the two men killed the lion because they wanted to sell its skin. Of course, this is against the law, but the hunter was more interested in all the money he could get for the lion skin. He wasn't really worried about the police. And the tourist was excited to see and kill a magnificent lion. Perhaps he could take a photograph, and tell his friends the story when he went home. He was a brave hunter!

It is difficult for the police or park officers to stop this killing. This time, the owner and the manager of the land where Batian was killed had to pay a fine (pay money to the government). But many animals are still killed, and three years later, another young lion was killed in the same way in the same area.

Lions in Danger

The Serengeti in Africa is probably the most famous national park in the world. This park is in Tanzania, and it is a huge wildlife reserve – in fact it is more than 9,000 square kilometres. Many wild animals live in the Serengeti, and usually they are safer there, inside the reserve. The Serengeti national park is especially important for lions, and about three thousand lions live there.

In the past, there were many more lions all over Africa, but now the number is much smaller. There are only about 100,000 left. Most of the lions today live on special animal reserves like the Serengeti. These reserves are very popular with tourists, because people can see the animals in their natural home when they visit the parks. And the lions and other animals are safer here, because park officers can try to look after them and protect them from hunters.

But hunters are not the only problem – there are many other dangers. In February 1994, a group of tourists were visiting the Serengeti reserve and watching the wildlife. The tourists were travelling above the ground in a hot air balloon. It was very exciting and everyone was looking down, pointing and taking photographs.

Suddenly, one of the tourists pointed his finger and shouted, "Look there! Something is wrong with that lion!". The others looked across and saw a lion lying on the ground. It was moving its legs slowly and trying to get up, but it couldn't stand up.

The pilot of the balloon worked in the national park, and he knew it was serious. He picked up his telephone and called the Serengeti's chief vet. The vet arrived quickly and examined the animal. But there was nothing the vet could do. The lion was very seriously ill and died that night.

Unfortunately, this was not the only lion to die like this. In the next few weeks, eleven more lions died in the same way. The vets in the park were very worried now, and at first they didn't know what was wrong. This was a new illness for them, and they didn't know how to stop it. The illness was spreading to the other lions in the reserve, and the vets watched as more and more of their big cats died. It was a disaster – in the next year, three thousand lions in the Serengeti died of this illness.

Then lions in the Masai Mara reserve in Kenya (a huge national park in the next country) started to get ill and die in the same way. Again, just like in the Serengeti, about one in three of the lions in the reserve died. The vets tried everything, but they needed money and expert help. "We have to do something quickly," agreed the scientists and vets, "or soon there will be no lions left in Africa".

Food for the pride

Lions often hunt large animals like buffalo, and one kill can give food for the whole pride (large group). The big male lions take most of the food, and sometimes there is nothing left for the cubs.

Finally, the scientists understood how the illness started. They explained that the lions were dying from a virus that you usually find in dogs. But how did the virus spread from the dogs to the big cats? Because wild dogs (hyenas and jackals) ate with the lions. The lions caught the virus from the wild dogs in the reserve. These dogs came to eat the meat of animals that the lions killed.

But the virus did not start with the hyenas and jackals, and it was unusual in wild animals. Scientists then found that the wild dogs got the virus from the guard dogs in the villages. Many local people lived in villages around the reserve. They had small farms, with some farm animals, and they kept guard dogs to look after their cattle. The virus didn't kill the guard dogs or the wild dogs, but it killed the big cats. The wild dogs caught the virus and passed it on to the big cats when they shared their food.

So now the scientists knew where the virus started, but this was not the end of the problem. How could they stop the deadly virus before it killed all the lions? The answer was simple. They gave injections to thousands of guard dogs around the Serengeti national park in a huge vaccination programme. This stopped the dogs from getting the disease, and then giving it to the wild hyenas and jackals. And it stopped the wild dogs passing it on.

Big Cats

When we think of big cat stories, we usually think of countries like Africa or Asia. But there are other stories of big cats around the world. One night in 1983, some farmers in Exmoor (a place in south-west England) got a big surprise. Something attacked and killed eighty of their sheep and young lambs. This was very strange, and they couldn't understand what had happened.

The farmers looked carefully at and around the dead animals for information. They saw some strange claw marks on the animals and footprints on the ground.

"It looks like a wild cat was here!" they said. But there were no native wild cats, and certainly no big cats in this area. "And how could one cat kill so many animals?" they asked.

The attacker bit the throats of the sheep – just like a big cat bites the throat of its prey. The farmers didn't find an answer to their questions that night, and the strange story appeared in the local newspaper. Since then, something has killed many more farm animals in Exmoor in the same way.

Although wild cats did live in England in the past, no big cats live naturally in this part of England today, so how is this story possible? Some experts think that they have a probable answer. Perhaps a big cat like a puma escaped from a zoo and started to live in the area. The local countryside in Exmoor is quite wild, with rocks, trees, and open spaces. It is a very good area for a big cat like a puma to live in, and it is possible for a cat to hunt and survive there. So perhaps the "zoo" story is a good explanation for the big cat on Exmoor.

A number of people say that they have seen a strange animal in the area, and now people call it the Beast of Exmoor. (A beast is a dangerous wild animal.) These stories are usually the same. People agree that the animal looks like a cat and it is about 1.2 metres long and 0.6 metres tall. It has a long tail and a dark-coloured coat.

One man who is sure he saw the Beast of Exmoor is called David Smith. David comes from a town near Exmoor, and he thinks that he came very close to the animal – almost face-to-face – when he was out hunting one day.

David liked hunting for rabbits with his dog, and often went out at weekends or in the evening. One day, while he was hunting, his dog went into some bushes (small trees) to look for the rabbits. Usually the dog frightened the rabbits, they ran out into the open, and David killed them. But this time the dog didn't find any rabbits. Both the dog and David got a big surprise!

Suddenly, an animal that looked like a big cat jumped out of the bushes. David couldn't believe his eyes – it was dark-coloured and looked very much like a puma! In a second, it ran past David and was gone. He had his gun in his hand, but he didn't shoot the big cat. "I was only there to hunt rabbits," he said, "I was really surprised when the big cat jumped out, but it didn't attack me and I didn't want to hurt it or kill it."

There are many stories like this about the strange big cat on Exmoor, and some people have tried to take photographs. Unfortunately, it is usually dark, or the beast is too far away, and the photographs are not very clear. At the moment, no-one really knows if there is (or was) a big cat there, and no-one really knows what killed all the sheep that night in 1983.

The World's Big Cats

Perhaps we do not know much about the life of the strange Beast of Exmoor, but we do know a lot about the other big cats in the world.

There are eight species of big cats: the lion, tiger, jaguar, leopard, snow leopard, clouded leopard, puma, and cheetah. All of them are carnivores, (meat-eaters). They all hunt in different ways, but there are two main ways that big cats catch their prey.

The first way of catching their prey is to chase (run after) the prey. Of course, to do this kind of hunting well, an animal has to be able to move very fast. The lion and the cheetah hunt in this way. In the lion pride the female lions do most of the hunting, and often work together in groups. The cheetah is the fastest of the big cats, and can run at speeds of 112 kilometres an hour. It usually hunts alone, and catches its prey after a short but very fast chase.

Other big cats ambush their prey. This means that they hide and wait before jumping out on their prey and killing it. Tigers, jaguars, pumas, and leopards usually hunt in this way.

Cheetah   *Puma*   *Jaguar*

The colours and markings on a big cat's coat are very important because they act as a kind of camouflage. This means that the colours are the same as the area behind them, and it is difficult for other animals to see them. This camouflage helps the cats to hide in the trees and long grass when they are hunting. The tiger has a striped orange and black coat. This makes it difficult to see in the long grasses of its home. The jaguar, cheetah, and leopards have spots. Lions and pumas have plain coats (only one colour), but when they are young, their cubs have spots. The spots make them difficult to see. This is very important as it helps to camouflage them and to protect them from other bigger (and more dangerous) animals.

Clouded leopard

Snow leopard

Leopard

Tiger

Lion

Glossary

ambush
A surprise attack where you hide and wait before jumping out and killing something.

camouflage
When the colour of an animal is the same as the area behind it.

claws
The hard nails on the end of a cat's fingers and toes.

cub
A young big cat.

den
A big cat's home.

extinct
When there are no animals of this kind left in the world.

hunt
To go after and kill an animal.

hyena
A wild animal like a dog that makes a noise like someone laughing.

injection
Putting something (like a medicine) into the blood, using a sharp needle.

jackal
A wild animal like a dog that lives in Asia and Africa.

jungle
Thick, forest areas in hot countries.

Masai Mara
A national park in Kenya, Africa.

national park
A special area used as a wildlife reserve.

prey
An animal that is caught and eaten by another animal.

pride
A group of lions.

rainforest
A tropical forest that gets a lot of rain.

reforestation
Planting trees to take the place of ones that have been cut down in a forest.

territory
An area of land where an animal lives.

vaccination
Putting something into the blood to protect the body from an illness, usually by injection.

vet (veterinary surgeon)
An animal doctor.

virus
A very small living thing that causes an illness or sickness and can pass very quickly from animal to animal (or person to person).

whiskers
The long hairs above a cat's mouth.

wildlife protection officer
Someone whose job is to look after animals on a reserve.

wildlife reserve
An area where wildlife is protected by special officers.